STATE PROFILES
WASHINGTON, D.C.

BY COLLEEN SEXTON

BELLWETHER MEDIA • MINNEAPOLIS, MN

Blastoff! Discovery launches a new mission: reading to learn. Filled with facts and features, each book offers you an exciting new world to explore!

This edition first published in 2022 by Bellwether Media, Inc.

No part of this publication may be reproduced in whole or in part without written permission of the publisher.
For information regarding permission, write to Bellwether Media, Inc.,
Attention: Permissions Department,
6012 Blue Circle Drive, Minnetonka, MN 55343.

Library of Congress Cataloging-in-Publication Data

Names: Sexton, Colleen A., 1967- author.
Title: Washington, D.C. / by Colleen Sexton.
Description: Minneapolis, MN : Bellwether Media, 2022. | Series:
   Blastoff! Discovery: State Profiles | Includes bibliographical
   references and index. | Audience: Ages 7-13 | Audience: Grades
   4-6 | Summary: "Engaging images accompany information about
   Washington, D.C. The combination of high-interest subject matter
   and narrative text is intended for students in grades 3 through 8"–
   Provided by publisher.
Identifiers: LCCN 2021020856 (print) | LCCN 2021020857
   (ebook) | ISBN 9781644873540 (library binding) | ISBN
   9781648341977 (ebook)
Subjects: LCSH: Washington (D.C.)–Juvenile literature.
Classification: LCC F194.3 .S48 2022 (print) | LCC F194.3 (ebook)
   | DDC 975.3–dc23
LC record available at https://lccn.loc.gov/2021020856
LC ebook record available at https://lccn.loc.gov/2021020857

Editor: Rebecca Sabelko   Designer: Brittany McIntosh

Printed in the United States of America, North Mankato, MN.

TABLE OF CONTENTS

The National Mall	4
Where Is Washington, D.C.?	6
Washington, D.C.'s, Beginnings	8
Landscape and Climate	10
Wildlife	12
People and Communities	14
Georgetown	16
Industry	18
Food	20
Sports and Entertainment	22
Festivals and Traditions	24
Washington, D.C., Timeline	26
Washington, D.C., Facts	28
Glossary	30
To Learn More	31
Index	32

THE NATIONAL MALL

WASHINGTON MONUMENT

It is a sunny spring morning in Washington, D.C. Students are touring the National Mall. The smell of cherry blossoms fills the air as they reach the Lincoln Memorial. They look up at the huge statue of President Abraham Lincoln.

AMERICA'S FRONT YARD

The National Mall is a narrow park that stretches about 2 miles (3 kilometers). It is sometimes called "America's Front Yard." More than 25 million people visit the Mall each year!

LIBRARY OF CONGRESS

MARTIN LUTHER KING, JR. MEMORIAL

ROCK CREEK PARK

THE WHITE HOUSE

The students walk beside the Reflecting Pool. The Washington Monument rises ahead. Inside, an elevator takes the students to the top. They see the city spread out below. The tour ends at the U.S. Capitol Building. Welcome to Washington, D.C.!

Washington, D.C., is the nation's capital. It is the home of the U.S. government. The city lies in the eastern United States. Maryland surrounds the capital on three sides. The Potomac River flows along the southwest border. It separates the capital from Virginia.

Washington, D.C., is not part of any state. The city lies in a **district** that covers around 68 square miles (176 square kilometers). Government buildings stand in the Capitol Hill neighborhood. Many other small neighborhoods fill the city. Some include Georgetown, Adams Morgan, and Foggy Bottom.

N
W + E
S

MARYLAND

WASHINGTON, D.C.

ADAMS MORGAN

GEORGETOWN

FOGGY BOTTOM

CAPITOL HILL

VIRGINIA

POTOMAC RIVER

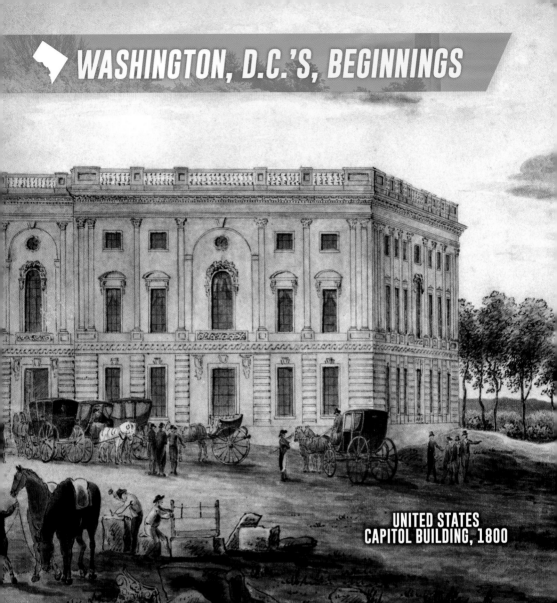

UNITED STATES
CAPITOL BUILDING, 1800

People first arrived in Washington, D.C., about 12,000 years ago. In time, the Nacotchtank people built villages. English explorers sailed up the Potomac River in 1608. English **colonists** later **settled** the region. They drove out the Nacotchtank. The colonists brought **enslaved** Africans to work in tobacco fields.

The United States needed a capital after the **Revolutionary War**. President George Washington chose the location in 1791. Enslaved people made up much of the labor force that built the first government buildings. When construction was finished in 1800, the government moved from Philadelphia to Washington, D.C.

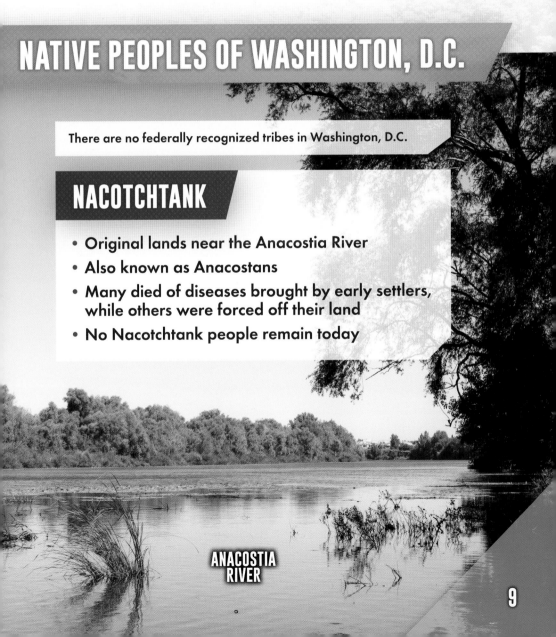

NATIVE PEOPLES OF WASHINGTON, D.C.

There are no federally recognized tribes in Washington, D.C.

NACOTCHTANK

- Original lands near the Anacostia River
- Also known as Anacostans
- Many died of diseases brought by early settlers, while others were forced off their land
- No Nacotchtank people remain today

ANACOSTIA RIVER

Most of Washington, D.C., stands on the Atlantic Coastal **Plain**. Low hills roll across the Piedmont region in the northwest. From there, the city slopes down to the Potomac River. The Anacostia River flows through the southeast to join the Potomac. The Tidal **Basin** near the Potomac was built to control flooding.

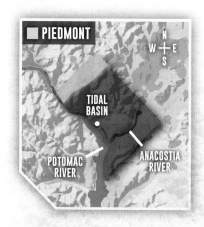

PIEDMONT

TIDAL BASIN

POTOMAC RIVER

ANACOSTIA RIVER

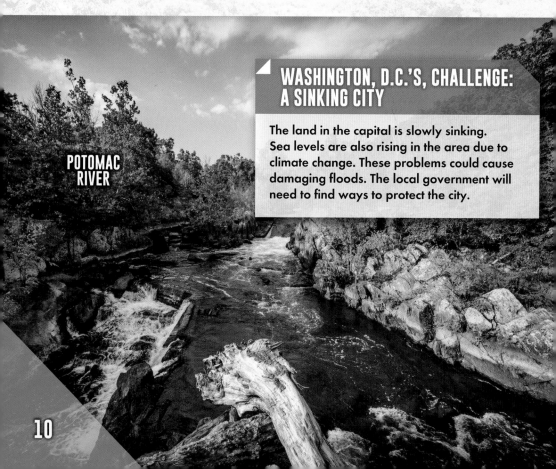

POTOMAC RIVER

WASHINGTON, D.C.'S, CHALLENGE: A SINKING CITY

The land in the capital is slowly sinking. Sea levels are also rising in the area due to climate change. These problems could cause damaging floods. The local government will need to find ways to protect the city.

SPRING
HIGH: 66°F (19°C)
LOW: 42°F (6°C)

SUMMER
HIGH: 87°F (31°C)
LOW: 65°F (18°C)

FALL
HIGH: 69°F (21°C)
LOW: 46°F (8°C)

WINTER
HIGH: 46°F (8°C)
LOW: 26°F (-3°C)

°F = degrees Fahrenheit
°C = degrees Celsius

TIDAL
BASIN

The capital is known for its hot and muggy summers.
Winters are mild and wet. Sometimes blizzards sweep in
with wind and snow. Residents enjoy mild temperatures in the
spring and fall.

WHITE-TAILED DEER

Washington, D.C.'s, parks are home to many animals. Deer dash between trees in Rock Creek Park. Gray squirrels race along branches. Coyotes prowl the forest for mice and snakes. Cardinals and goldfinches sing from the treetops.

COYOTE

Raccoons and opossums creep through the city's streets. They search for food at night. Bats gobble up insects. Red-tailed hawks and bald eagles grab fish from rivers. Great blue herons and snowy egrets wade in shallow water. Eastern box turtles take in the sun near streams and ponds.

VIRGINIA OPOSSUMS

SNOWY EGRET

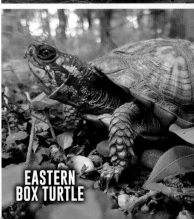
EASTERN BOX TURTLE

A BIRD'S-EYE VIEW

The capital is home to a famous bald eagle pair. Mr. President and the First Lady live near the Anacostia River. Their young are named Freedom and Liberty!

BALD EAGLE

Life Span: up to 28 years
Status: least concern

bald eagle range =

LEAST CONCERN	NEAR THREATENED	VULNERABLE	ENDANGERED	CRITICALLY ENDANGERED	EXTINCT IN THE WILD	EXTINCT

Around 689,000 people live in Washington, D.C. The capital is part of a **metropolitan** area of more than 6 million people. It includes the cities of Arlington and Alexandria in Virginia. Parts of Maryland are also included.

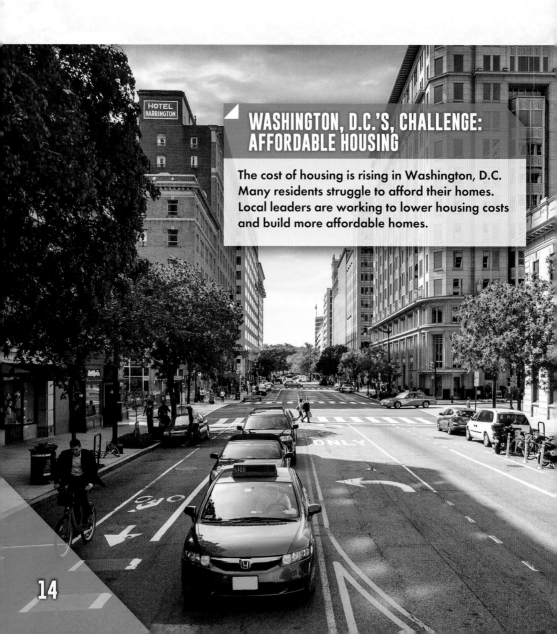

WASHINGTON, D.C.'S, CHALLENGE: AFFORDABLE HOUSING

The cost of housing is rising in Washington, D.C. Many residents struggle to afford their homes. Local leaders are working to lower housing costs and build more affordable homes.

FAMOUS WASHINGTONIAN

Name: Bill Nye

Born: November 27, 1955

Hometown: Washington, D.C.

Famous For: Taught the importance of science in day-to-day life through his television programs that included *Bill Nye the Science Guy* and *Bill Nye Saves the World*

Nearly half of all Washingtonians are African American or Black. Around 4 in 10 are white with European backgrounds. Just over 1 in 10 residents is Hispanic. Smaller numbers of Native Americans and Asian Americans live in the city. Newcomers have arrived from El Salvador, Ethiopia, Trinidad and Tobago, China, and Mexico.

15

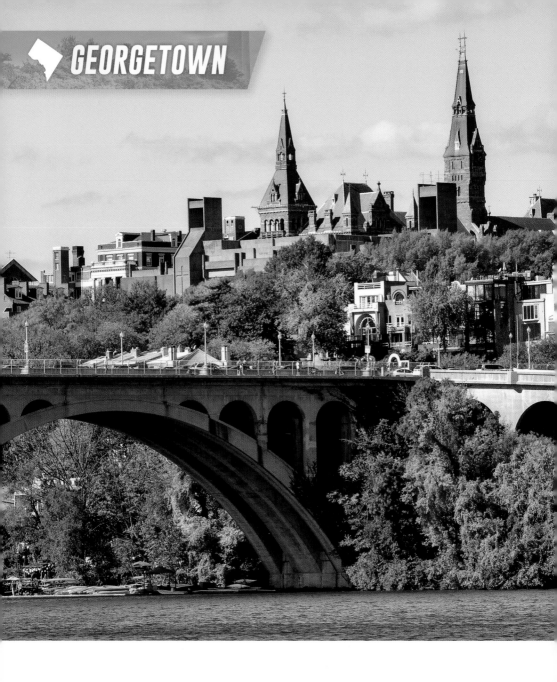

Georgetown is a historic neighborhood. It was founded in 1751 in Maryland. It grew into a busy port on the Potomac River. The settlement became part of the capital in 1791. Today, it is known for its grand houses and tree-lined streets. It is also home to Georgetown University.

Georgetown's residents enjoy biking and picnics along the Chesapeake and Ohio **Canal**. They head to Book Hill for its art galleries, antique stores, and cafés. Shoppers browse the trendy shops on M Street. Summer river cruises begin at Georgetown Waterfront Park. Washington Harbour Ice Rink draws ice skaters in winter. It has the city's largest outdoor rink!

CHESAPEAKE AND OHIO CANAL

WATERFRONT PARK

INSIDE THE
U.S. CAPITOL BUILDING

The U.S. government is the largest employer in Washington, D.C. Government officials hold the best-known jobs. Thousands of other people work in government offices. Other Washingtonians work for newspapers, magazines, or book publishers. Some work at the district's many colleges and universities.

THE SMITHSONIAN

The Smithsonian Institution includes 19 museums and the National Zoo. Visitors explore the natural world, art, and the history of flight. They also learn about the history of Native Americans and African Americans.

Many Washingtonians work in banks, law firms, and hospitals. The district's millions of visitors each year make **tourism** an important **service industry**. Museums and historic sites employ tour guides. Other workers welcome tourists to hotels and restaurants.

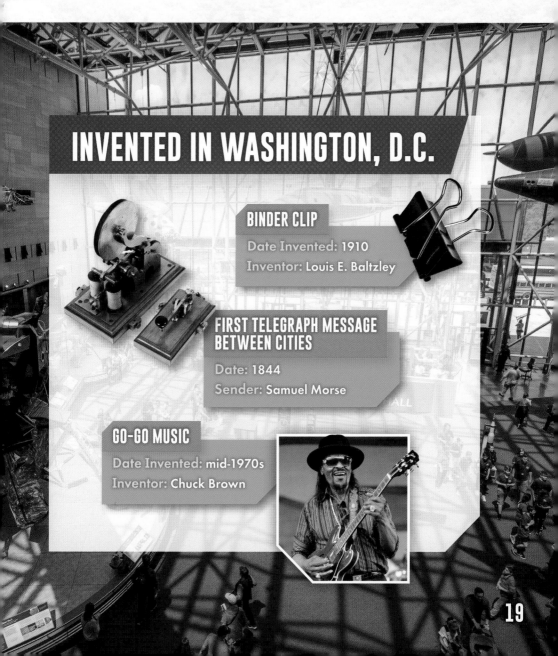

INVENTED IN WASHINGTON, D.C.

BINDER CLIP
Date Invented: 1910
Inventor: Louis E. Baltzley

FIRST TELEGRAPH MESSAGE BETWEEN CITIES
Date: 1844
Sender: Samuel Morse

GO-GO MUSIC
Date Invented: mid-1970s
Inventor: Chuck Brown

HALF-SMOKE

SOUP'S ON!

Senate bean soup has been on the U.S. Senate dining room menu for more than 100 years! It features navy beans, ham, and onions.

Washingtonians enjoy burgers and many other classic American foods. The half-smoke is a local favorite. This smoked pork and beef sausage is served on a bun with onions, chili, and cheese. Cooks serve up crabs and oysters from the nearby Chesapeake Bay. Sweet and tangy mumbo sauce is a popular topping for chicken wings and french fries.

Immigrants have brought their own flavors to the city. Korean fried chicken features a crunchy crust topped with a spicy sauce. Peruvian **rotisserie** chicken is also popular. *Pupusas* have roots in El Salvador and Honduras. Cooks stuff these cornmeal flatbreads with cheese, meat, and beans.

KOREAN FRIED CHICKEN

PUPUSAS

MUMBO SAUCE

4 SERVINGS

Have an adult help you make this recipe!

INGREDIENTS

1/2 cup tomato paste
1 cup distilled white vinegar
1 cup pineapple or orange juice
1 cup sugar
4 teaspoons soy sauce
1 teaspoon powdered ginger
1/4 teaspoon hot sauce

DIRECTIONS

1. Mix all the ingredients in a pot.

2. Simmer, but do not boil, for about 20 minutes.

3. Taste and add more of any ingredient you would like.

4. Serve warm or at room temperature with chicken wings or french fries.

Washington, D.C., is a center for **culture**. Residents tour the city's many museums and historic sites. They enjoy plays at the National Theatre and Ford's Theatre. Symphony, ballet, and opera performances draw crowds to the Kennedy Center. Many Washingtonians take in live music around the city.

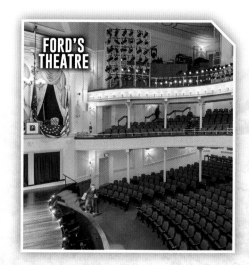

FORD'S THEATRE

22

Sports fans have a lot to cheer for. Many root for the city's professional football, baseball, and basketball teams. Hockey and soccer games also draw big crowds. Hikers and bikers follow trails in the city's many parks. Boaters enjoy sunny days on the Potomac River. The National Zoo draws many families.

ROCK CREEK PARK

Rock Creek Park in northwestern Washington, D.C., is one of the country's largest city parks. Residents can hike trails, go horseback riding, and play golf. The park also includes a nature center and a planetarium.

NOTABLE SPORTS TEAM

Washington Mystics
Sport: Women's National Basketball Association
Started: 1998
Place of Play: Entertainment and Sports Arena

Washingtonians celebrate spring with the National Cherry Blossom Festival. Kite flying and a parade welcome big crowds. Marching bands wind through the streets to celebrate DC **Emancipation** Day every April 16. It honors the day enslaved Africans in the capital were freed.

Embassies open their doors for tours during Passport DC in May. In summer, the National Mall hosts the Smithsonian Folklife Festival. People of all backgrounds celebrate their roots with **traditional** music, dance, and arts. Every Fourth of July, crowds fill the National Mall to watch fireworks light up the sky over the nation's capital. There is a lot to celebrate in Washington, D.C.!

A GATHERING PLACE

The National Mall is an important public space for celebrations and protests. Martin Luther King, Jr. gave his famous "I Have a Dream" speech there during the 1963 March on Washington.

KITE FLYING DURING THE
NATIONAL CHERRY BLOSSOM FESTIVAL

25

1800

The nation's capital is moved to Washington, D.C.

1608

English explorers led by Captain John Smith sail up the Potomac River

1865

President Abraham Lincoln is shot in Ford's Theatre

1751

Georgetown is founded

1814

During the War of 1812, British troops burn much of Washington, D.C., including the White House, the U.S. Capitol, and other government buildings

2020

The city's professional football team announces that it will change its name in response to calls for racial justice

1963

Martin Luther King, Jr. delivers his "I Have a Dream" speech at the Lincoln Memorial

1964

Washingtonians gain the right to vote in presidential elections

2016

The National Museum of African American History and Culture, the country's first national museum to focus on the African American experience, opens on the National Mall

2021

Congress begins voting on a bill to grant the District of Columbia statehood

Nicknames: D.C., The District, The Nation's Capital

Motto: *Justitia Omnibus* (Justice for All)

Date Founded: July 16, 1790

Area: around 68 square miles (176 square kilometers)

Population

689,545
(2020)

DISTRICT FLAG

The Washington, D.C., flag was adopted in 1938. It is based on George Washington's coat of arms. It features a row of three red stars and two red stripes on a white background.

INDUSTRY

JOBS

- MANUFACTURING **1%**
- FARMING AND NATURAL RESOURCES **1%**
- GOVERNMENT **21%**
- SERVICES **77%**

Main Exports

aircraft parts

machine parts

ammunition

weapons

Natural Resources

GOVERNMENT

Federal Government

1 DELEGATE | **0** SENATORS

DC

3 ELECTORAL VOTES

USA

District Government

MAYOR, CITY ADMINISTRATOR | **13** COUNCIL MEMBERS

DISTRICT SYMBOLS

DISTRICT BIRD
WOOD THRUSH

DISTRICT FRUIT
CHERRY

DISTRICT FLOWER
AMERICAN BEAUTY ROSE

DISTRICT TREE
SCARLET OAK

GLOSSARY

basin—the area drained by a river

canal—a human-made waterway that boats can travel through

colonists—people sent by a government to a new region or territory

culture—the beliefs, arts, and ways of life in a place or society

district—an area or region

emancipation—the act of setting someone free from control or slavery

embassies—the official residences of ambassadors from foreign countries

enslaved—to be considered property and forced to work for no pay

immigrants—people who move to a new country

metropolitan—the combined city and suburban area

plain—a large area of flat land

Revolutionary War—the war from 1775 to 1783 in which the United States fought for independence from Great Britain

rotisserie—related to food that is cooked by rotating it over a fire or other source of heat

service industry—a group of businesses that perform tasks for people or other businesses

settled—moved somewhere and made it home

tourism—the business of people traveling to visit other places

traditional—related to customs, ideas, or beliefs handed down from one generation to the next

TO LEARN MORE

AT THE LIBRARY

Kellaher, Karen. *Washington, D.C.* New York, N.Y.: Children's Press, 2018.

Kelley, Kitty. *Martin's Dream Day.* New York, N.Y.: Atheneum Books for Young Readers, 2017.

Schroeder, Alan. *Washington, D.C.: Our Nation's Capital from A–Z.* New York, N.Y.: Holiday House, 2018.

ON THE WEB

FACTSURFER

Factsurfer.com gives you a safe, fun way to find more information.

1. Go to www.factsurfer.com.

2. Enter "Washington, D.C." into the search box and click 🔍.

3. Select your book cover to see a list of related content.

INDEX

Adams Morgan, 6, 7

Anacostia River, 9, 10, 13

arts, 17, 22, 24

Capitol Hill, 6, 7

challenges, 10, 14

climate, 10, 11

DC Emancipation Day, 24

fast facts, 28-29

festivals, 24-25

Foggy Bottom, 6, 7

food, 20-21

Fourth of July, 24

Georgetown, 6, 7, 16-17

history, 8-9, 16, 24

inventions, 19

King, Martin Luther, Jr., 24

landmarks, 4, 5, 8, 12, 16, 17, 18, 22, 23

landscape, 6, 7, 8, 9, 10-11, 12, 16, 20, 23

location, 6-7, 9

National Cherry Blossom Festival, 24, 25

National Mall, 4-5, 24

Nye, Bill, 15

outdoor activities, 17, 23, 24, 25

Passport DC, 24

people, 8, 9, 14-15, 18, 21, 24

Potomac River, 6, 7, 8, 10, 16, 23

recipe, 21

Revolutionary War, 9

size, 6

Smithsonian Folklife Festival, 24

sports, 23

timeline, 26-27

Washington, George, 9

Washington Mystics, 23

wildlife, 12-13

working, 8, 9, 18-19